MINISTRY OF DEACONS IN URBAN AMERICA

Διακονοσ

A Ministry of Compassion
And Helpfulness

John D. Brinson

Resource *Publications*
An imprint of *Wipf and Stock Publishers*
199 West 8th Avenue • Eugene OR 97401

Resource Publications
An imprint of Wipf & Stock Publishers
199 West 8th, Suite 3
Eugene, OR 97401

Ministry of Deacons in Urban America
By Brinson, John D.
Copyright©2003 by Brinson, John D.
ISBN: 1-59244-437-7

Publication date 12/12/2003

Preface

We Christians are blessed because we have God's Holy Bible to guide us when we are confronted with a problem and need an answer. It doesn't matter what the problem is, God has supplied the answer in the Holy Bible, and especially in matters that affect the Church.

There is a misunderstanding in many congregations about the ministry of deacons. Because of this misunderstanding, conflict has occurred within many of our congregations between the pastorate and diaconate.

In all things that affect our lives we need to read the Holy Bible and find out what God has to say about the issues. If we continue to build on man's opinions and traditions, we will be building on sinking sand.

The information in this book is composed of facts gathered from research of the Holy Bible; Church documents; writings of Church fathers, and modern theologians.

My fondest dream is that this information will contribute in some small way to help the pastorate, the diaconate, and members of the congregation better understand the role of the deacons.

Rev. John D Brinson, M/Div.

iv

Contents

Preface	iii
Introduction	vii
Deacons and The Primitive Church	1
Deacons and The Middle Age Period	13
Deacons and The Reformation Period	17
Women and The Diaconate	19
Prerequisites and Qualifications	29
Urban Ministries	35
Notable Deacons of The Past	49
Role of a Mothers' Board	51
Stewardship Parables of Jesus Christ	60
How to Succeed in Christian Life	60
Questions to Answer	61
Training Program	63
Basic Guide To Institution Visitation	65
Bibliography	67

vi

Introduction

To really appreciate a book, it helps to know a little of the noble background of the author. I have known Rev. John Brinson for many years and he is not one who would carelessly throw something together in order to produce a book. He is a high achiever and a polished scholar. John has made a disciplined, thoughtful, and rigorous effort to present an elegant writing in the book, "M*inistry of Deacons in Urban America."* This qualitative book is a must for pastors, ministers, deacons and laity in both urban and suburban church settings. However, I feel it will be especially effective to churches with a congregational polity. Even though the circumstances in autonomous churches differ, much of what happens in ministry between pastors, deacons and parishioners, is more or less linked together. Generally what is helpful in one autonomous church works in most Congregational Churches. *"Ministry of Deacons in Urban America"* is written in detail and provides many solutions to problems that transpire between pastors and deacons as well as between parishioners and deacons. John has presented ideas that are logical and pragmatic. Not only has he used the Bible and history well, but also some of his experience and the experiences of other pastors. He does not elude controversial issues but faces them with courage and convictions. He gives deep devotion to biblical principles in his presentations. Included in this book is a multitude of information that has been used by me in my local church. It contains healthy instruction as well as information that will help the deacon in his devotional time, family life, and in various areas of ministry. Rev. Brinson gives a practical and historical look at deacon ministry from Biblical times to the present. Hopefully his writing will help to create better understanding and relationships between pastors, deacons and lay church members everywhere.

Dr. Theodore P. Fields
Pastor of New Hope Baptist Church
Union City, California

Chapter 1

Deacons
And The Primitive Church

We shall begin by defining the Greek words used in the New Testament and associated with deacons, and their works.

1.**Diakonos** (n) One who ministers, it originally meant a waiter, or servant.

2.**Diakonein** (v) means, to serve. It is the New Testament word for the act of ministry.

3.**Diakonia** (n) means, ministry, the name of the act.

All Christians are ministers (servants) in Christ. Our ministry is by definition, one of service. Christ declares:

> *For even the Son of Man came not to be ministered unto but to minister and give his life a ransom for many.*[1]

Christ is our supreme example. We are to emulate him as we carry on his ministry in the world. Because he came to serve and not be served, as his disciples we too, must serve as opposed to being served. Christ confirms this as he says:

---

[1] *Matt* 20:28

> ...So shall it be among you: but whoever will be great among you, shall be your minister.[2]

One of the great ministries in the church is that performed by those who are members of the deacons' office. They function as pastor's assistants, and are used in various ministries according to their personal gifts and graces. The diaconate is distinct as one of the oldest offices in the Christian church. They are mentioned in the New Testament as close associates to the bishops (see Philippians 1:1, and 1 Timothy 3:8, 12).

Acts 6:1-6, is traditionally accepted as a description of the origin of the office of deacon. The words diakonia (ministry), and diakonein (to serve) are found there, but there is no reference at all to an office. This passage describes a function, but does not indicate an office.

The first time the term for deacons as an office (diakonos) is used, is in Paul's first letter to Timothy. This passage lists the qualifications for deacons, but it does not indicate which ministries deacons are appointed to perform.

> *Likewise must the deacons be grave, not double-tongued, not given to much wine, not greedy of filthy lucre. 9.holding the mystery of the faith in pure conscience. 10.And let these also be proved; then let them use the office of deacon, being found blameless...12.let the deacons be the husbands of one wife, ruling their children and their own houses well. 13.For they that have used the office of a deacon well purchase to themselves a good degree, and great boldness in the faith, which is in Jesus Christ.[3]*

---

[2] *ibid.*, 20:26.
[3] 1*Tim* 3:8-13.

In the above passage the term for office (diakonos) is used. It appears that when first appointed to this special service, deacons (servants) were involved in a ministry without the benefit of an official office. It appears that the apostles originally set the *seven* aside to perform a special ministry of waiting on the tables of the Greek widows, and perhaps later as their ministries began to evolve they were delegated an office. It is significant that the apostle Paul used the word deacon in its functional sense when referring to them rather than as an office.

The word, diakonos is of Greek origin, and means minister or servant. Consequently, a deacon is a servant. But aren't all Christians servants? Yes, **all** Christians are servants, but according to Holy Scripture they have different areas, and levels of responsibility.

Let's take a brief survey of some of these areas, levels, and responsibilities:

Pastors are ministers (servants) of Jesus Christ, or the Word of God. In his instructions to Timothy, as recorded in 1 Timothy, Paul writes as follows:

> *If thou put the brethren in remembrance of these things, thou shall be a good minister of Jesus Christ, nourished up in the words of faith and good doctrine, whereunto thou hast attained.*[4]

Paul explicitly states in the above passage that pastors are ministers of Jesus Christ. In his letter to the church at Rome he states the following.

---

[4] *ibid.*, 4:6.

> *That I should be a minister of Jesus Christ to the Gentiles, ministering the gospel of God, that the offering up of the Gentiles might be acceptable, being sanctified by the Holy Ghost.*[5]

We can ascertain from the above two passages that according to Paul, pastors (preachers, ministers) are called by God to be ministers of his Incarnated Holy Word. Pastors are not ministers of the church, because the church does not call pastors to their ministry, but they are called by God to be ministers of his Holy Word. Congregations with the Holy Spirit decide which minister will oversee which congregation.

Deacons are ministers (servants) of the church, because it is the church that calls them. According to the writer of the book of Acts, the twelve commanded the congregation to,

> *...Look ye out among you seven men...whom we may appoint over this business.*[6]

According to Acts, the congregation chose the original "seven", but they were appointed by the "twelve" to their ministry, which was waiting the tables of the widows.

In his letter to the church in Rome, in support of Phoebe, Paul asserts they are servants (ministers) of the church.

> *I commend to you Phoebe our sister, which is a servant of the church at Cenchrea; ...*[7]

So, we can discern from the above passages that deacons are chosen by the congregation, and appointed to their ministries to the congregation by the pastor.

---

[5]*Rom 15:16.*
[6]*Acts 6:2,3.*
[7]*Rom 15:16*

Members of the congregation are ministers (servants) of each other as believers in Jesus Christ, who says,

> *Love ye one another, as I have loved You.*[8]

And in the Gospel of Mark we are reminded,

> *And he sat down, and called the twelve, ... and saith unto them, if any man desire to be first, the same shall be last of all, and servant of all.*[9]

From the beginning the ministry of the deacons was service to the congregation. If indeed their beginning is recorded in Acts, their original ministry was to serve the tables of the needy. This has evolved into our current acts of benevolence. But very early on their ministry began to expand, and their various gifts began to be used in ministries that contributed greatly to the church. Some of these gifts according to the book of Acts were as follows:

1. Miracles and works of wonder,

> And Stephen, full of faith and power, did great wonders and miracles among the people.[10]

2. Preaching and wisdom,

> And they were not able to resist the wisdom and the spirit by which he spake.[11]

3. Evangelism,

---

[8] *John* 15:12
[9] *Mark* 10:43
[10] *Acts* 6:8
[11] *Acts* 6:10

> And the next day we that were of Paul's company departed, and came unto Caesarea: and we entered into the house of Philip the Evangelist, which was one of the seven, and abode with him.[12]

The seventh chapter of Acts is the account of Deacon Stephen's preaching. His preaching was so powerful *"they were cut to the heart"*...and they *"stopped their ears"*[13]. He was a notable preacher. He also has the distinction of being the first deacon-preacher-martyr for the Christian cause.[14]

Philip being full of the Holy Spirit, baptized the Ethiopian official,[15] and preached in all the "cities from Azotus to Caesarea."[16] Paul was destroying churches and persecuting Christians during this period and as a consequence, Philip was amongst those dispersed by Paul and his troops. Philip has the distinction of being the first to preach the gospel in Samaria. He was full of the Holy Spirit and was used in a great way for our Lord. Now, this is the same Philip that was set-aside with the seven men in Acts to serve the congregation as deacons.

Let us observe what the church father, Eusebius informs us about Philip and his power of persuasion in proclaiming the gospel of Jesus Christ.

> *So great was the divine grace working with him that even Simon the Magus with very many others was won over by his words. Such a name had Simon obtained at that time by the sorceries with which he got his dupes into his power that he was believed to be the Great Power of God, but now even he was struck dumb by the miracles that Philip performed*

---

[12] *Acts* 21:8
[13] *Acts* 7:54.
[14] *Acts* 7:1-53
[15] *ibid.*, 8:38.
[16] *ibid.*, 8:40.

> by divine power, and slipped in: he actually received baptism, in his hypocritical pretence of belief in Christ.[17]

There is the possibility that the character and the preaching of Stephen influenced Paul. His speech was the first missionary preaching delivered before the Sanhedrin. Stephen made the analogous point in his proclamation that the people of Israel were destroying the representatives of God, just as the Jewish leaders had rejected and crucified Jesus Christ. He made a powerful and fearless address for the cause of Christianity before its oppressive enemies.

Now, this was the same Philip and Stephen the congregation had selected and the apostles had set aside to serve the tables of the widows. The church's rapid growth brought problems in the management of its programs, so the *seven* had been appointed to assist the overseers in managing the ministries to the church. Stephen and Philip are evidence that deacons were used ministries other than benevolent. They began to be used according to the gifts and grace that were evidenced in them.

It can be argued that Stephen's speech before the Sanhedrin acted as a catalyst on Paul's conscience. It contributed greatly to Paul's meeting with our Lord on the road to Damascus, and his conversion. If this is the case then we can say that it is because of this deacon's powerful and Spirit filled preaching that Paul's participation in the destruction of churches and persecution of Christians came to an end. Paul was present at the execution of Stephen.[18]

What is the ministry of deacons? Are they ordained to serve tables exclusively? Has not Holy Scripture, and the writings of the church fathers plainly shown that they were used in many other ministries of the church. While we must admit that the

---

[17]Eusebius. *The History of the Church*. pp. 73,74.
[18] *Acts* 26:10

primary responsibility of deacons during the first couple of centuries after Christ was serving the needy members of the congregation, some nevertheless rose to power and prominence by assisting the overseer in preaching and other areas.

It appears that Acts 6:1-6, describes the beginning of the ministry of deacons, but it is not a *chiseled in stone* account of the limitations of their ministry. As we have seen, deacons were used in various ministries, as the churches needs determined. The overseers would use them according to their talents, and the grace bestowed upon them by the Holy Spirit.

Deacons performed administrative assignments, kept order in the church, administered church funds, participated in worship (assisted in baptism, and the Lord's Supper), did evangelism, mission, and provided for the social welfare of the members of the Roman Church. There were no trustees, clerks, and various others we designate as officers of the church. Trustees are really later additions, that can really be defined as agents of the state and IRS. When the church and state split, trustees were required by the government to protect the state's interests.* The function of trustees is to manage the wealth of the church, and provide the state with its taxes, etc. The New Testament based church has only two offices, and they are; the pastorate and diaconate.

Many churches take the position that deacons are appointed to serve the tables of the widows (benevolence), and nothing more. But they must come to terms with Philips and Stephens evangelism and preaching, and Philip's baptism of the Ethiopian official.

In the birth of deacons they were appointed to a table-serving ministry, but early in the childhood of this ministry as they began to grow in grace and talent their responsibilities began to expand into other realms. Philip and Stephen evidenced this. So we note

---

* The Trustee Board is not a spiritual office. The spiritual church has only two offices, clergy and deacons. Trustees are officers of the corporation and are entrusted with stewardship of the spiritual church's property.

that in the primitive church deacons practiced both a spiritual and temporal ministry. They were committed to their ministries. Stephen was martyred because of his ministry, and went to glory preaching Christ crucified to the enemies of the gospel.

In Acts their ministry of compassion is depicted as they tended the sick and afflicted.

> *For unclean spirits, crying with loud voice, came out of many that were possessed with them: and many taken with palsies, and that were lame, were healed.*[19]

Deweese reports an eyewitness described them during the plague of Alexandria as,

> *Those who visited the sick fearlessly... ministered to them continually, and died with them most joyfully.*[20]

The deacons of the primitive church were functional in their appointments to church service. They performed many works and these works were bounded where the duties of the pastor began, and where their gifts and graces were not adequate.

Let me summarize my remarks by saying deacons evidently have their origin in the appointment and ordination of the seven men with the Grecian names in Acts 6:1-6. They were originally appointed to serve the tables of the widows, but as the church continued to grow and its needs expanded, the apostles assigned them to other ministries according to their gifts.

Deacons are ministers, as all members of the body of Christ by definition are ministers. We are all servants, just as our master, Jesus Christ considered himself a servant.

---

[19] *Acts* 8:7.
[20] Charles Deweese. *Emerging Role of Deacons*. Nashville: 1979 Pp. 12,13.

> *Ye call me master and Lord: and ye say well; for so I am. If I then, your Lord and master, have washed your feet; ye also ought to wash one another's feet. For I have given you an example that ye should do as I have done to you.*[21]

The role of deacons according to the Bible is one of servant to church and community. Throughout the history of deacons the form of their ministry has been determined by the church and confirmed by the pastor. Depending on the church or congregation and its needs, a functional diaconal ministry should be in place. Now, we must all understand that what may be functional and relevant in one class of church, may not be functional, or relevant in another. For instance, a church that serves the needs of a community of the rich, ruling class should not have the same needs as a church in the community of the poor, downtrodden people of the ghetto.

The rich man and Lazarus both needed the salvation Christ offers, but they had different worldly needs.

The information given and the references cited above, hopefully throws some light on the origin of deacons, and the varied ministries they were involved with in the primitive church. This period roughly covers the time span from A.D.30 to A.D. 325. During this period, the focus of the church's theology was on the sacramental person, and the functional ministry was of those who in word and their actions embodied Christ. The people had confidence in and expected great things from the representative of Christ. Leaders tend to self fulfill these expectancies. Let me explain. We have in our midst today, many healing ministries brought to us by television. These leaders perform healing ministries before our very eyes. They develop this ability because

---

[21]*John* 13:15.

their adherents conceive them as sacramental persons. Consequently, miracles are expected, and miracles occur.

During this period deacons were healers, preachers, miracle workers, treasurers, and civil servants of the local congregations. They were also engaged in a ministry of compassion and, benevolence. The church was the recipient of many blessed, ministries from its deacons during this period. Theirs were not ministries that ended within the walls of the sanctuaries, but extended into the streets of Alexandria, in caring for those persons suffering from the terrible plague.

This period was one of glory for those in the diaconate. Professor Urban Holmes III notes the following about the function of primitive church deacons.

> *They have liturgical functions and administer charity (Trallians 2:3); They preach and go out as missionaries (Philadelphians 10:1); and they are consulted as a body by laymen before anything can be done (Trallians 7:4).*[22]

Deacons were administrators of "the offerings, and of all the temporal concerns of the churches," according to the notes in the History of the First Council of Nice. These notes also mention, "The poor received alms from their hands, and the clergy their stipends and remuneration."[23] During this period they practiced benevolence to the destitute, and distributed the paychecks to the clergy.

This glorious period did not last very long. When the church changed its theological focus, it impacted directly on the deacon ministries. The goals of deacons began to change and the diaconate glory began to fade into obscurity.

---

[22]Urban T. Holmes. *The Future Shape of Ministry* (N.Y., 1971), p.25.
[23]*History of the First Council of Nice* (N.Y., 1992), p.106.

Chapter 2

Deacons And
The Middle Age Period

During the middle age (A.D. 325-A.D. 1517), there was a decline in the types of ministries that deacons were involved in. This decline occurred because the focus of the church's theology changed, and impacted on the goals of those in the diaconate. The church's theology up to this period was focused on the sacramental person. The person doing ministry was eschatological, he had his existence within a persecuted community, but transcended it, and stood at the edge of an alternate reality. He was in a sense answering the call of Christ to be a participant in the kingdom of heaven. He embodied the spirit of Christ in his person.

This theological focus however gave way to a new theology based on the sacramental rite. The Roman Empire had come to an end and brought with it an influx of Germanic tribes.[24] The church had to redefine its faith in this changing world in the context of feudalism, Platonism, and the German religious perspective. The Germanic people were animistic in their world view. This outlook provided for the reality of demons and devils, etc., and the Mass became the door into the new alternative reality. The Church's theology focused on the sacramental rite.

During this period many of these new people were added to the church's membership. With this growth, the areas over which bishops presided took in more people than the bishops could manage productively. During this time priests made their

---

[24]Urban T. Holmes. *The Future Shape of Ministry* (N.Y.,1971), p.38.

appearance on the scene. Their primary function was to preside over a smaller section of the bishop's domain, thereby relieving the bishop of some of the pressures of his many responsibilities.

Now that the church's faith focused on ritual, rather than the eschatological person, the deacons began to shift their ministry towards a liturgical function. During this period many deacons left the diaconate to move up the hierarchical ladder of church beaurocracy. For many the diaconate primarily degenerated to function as a mere step in the rungs of the ladder to the priesthood. They certainly had moved in a very different position from Paul's definition of the diaconate as functional. Their primary interest now, was on the office of priesthood. This office became the objective goal of more than a few deacons, who moved up through the ranks of the diaconate and lesser ministries to become ordained priests.[25]

This practice prompted George Williams to claim that the office of deacons,

> *could no longer be considered a terminal or life ministry. It was merely a rung in the clerical ladder.*[26]

It was the beginning of the middle age, at the Council of Nice (AD 325), that the church resolved to re-define the ministry of the diaconate. This also signaled the beginning of the decline of the glory of the diaconate. Recorded below are the words issued by the Council in respect to deacons and their relationship to bishops and presbyters.

> *It having come to the knowledge of the great and holy Council, that, in certain places and cities, the*

---

[25]Ibid., p.39.
[26]G.H. Williams. *Ministry of the Later patristic Period (314-451), The Ministry in Historical Perspective* (N.Y.,1956), p.63.

> Eucharist is administered, by deacons, to presbyters, and neither law nor custom permitting that those, who have no authority to offer the body of Christ, should deliver it to those who have; and it being also understood, that some deacons receive the Eucharist before even the bishops, let therefore, all these irregularities be removed, and let the deacons remain within their own limits, knowing they are ministers of the bishops, and inferior to the presbyters. Let them receive the Eucharist in their proper place, after the presbyters, whether it be administered by a bishop or presbyter. Nor is if permitted to deacons to sit among the presbyters, as that is against the rule and order. If any one will not obey, even after these regulations, let him desist from his ministry.[27]

Admittedly, this was an awful blow to the glory of the diaconate ministry, but it was the temptation to move up the ecclesiastical ladder and become priests that stand out in bold relief as the straw that broke the camel's back.

The ministry of the diaconate had begun its downward spiral and continued until it reached a point where it was unrecognizable in the context of a viable ministry, and finally ends. A ministry that had once flourished with glory now had become ineffective and non-existent.

Professor Urban T Holmes, reports the following to us on the state of deacon ministry around the thirteenth century:

> The diaconate disappears after the twelfth and thirteenth centuries, despite all efforts to revive it, as a significant realm of ministerial function.[28]

---

[27] *History of the Council of Nice* (N.Y.,1992), p.106.
[28] Urban T. Holmes. *The Future Shape of Ministry* (N.Y.,1971), p.95

After this fall into obscurity, the diaconate ceased to be a functioning reality for several centuries.

The church once again changed the focus of its theology. Its theological focus shifted from the sacramental rite to the sacramental word. In this new approach to church theology, the sacramental word became the incarnated expression of our Lord's ministry, even when it was motivated to touch the emotions, and not necessarily the mind.

With this new theological focus of the church, came the opportunity for revival of the diaconate, and its ministries. The church now found itself in the midst of a rapidly changing culture; technology was now impacting on the "western man" in such a way that he became aware of his ability to reason cognitively. Western man began to organize things around the order of reason and the printed word. In a sense we could say that the Guttenberg press helped to usher in a revival of the diaconate.

Chapter 3

Deacons And
The Reformation Period

With the Protestant Reformation came the change in the church's theology to the Word as sacrament. This was the beginning of the age of the printed word. With the printed word came an understanding of the power of reason and nationalism. Technology created a middle class that practiced among other things, the protestant work ethic, and family values. Within this context, the sacramental word was the new theological focus of the church.

It was in this context that new ideas about the role and function of deacons began to come to light. This period saw the end of the overriding influence of ritual, and deacons' efforts to become a part of the priesthood.

In the Confession of Faith of the Anabaptist, in the year A. D. 1580, there is the implication that deacons were once again becoming a vital part of the church. C.W. DeWeese advises us,

> *The early Anabaptist-Mennonite movement universally established the office of Deacon as an important ordained office.*[29]

During the 17th century, deacons were beginning to make their mark as a functional part of the Baptist Churches in America. They are mentioned and recorded in the minutes of the First Baptist Church in Boston, during the mid-seventh century

---

[29]Charles.DeWeese. *The Emerging Role of Deacons* (Nashville,1979),p.20.

(1660's). They were also a stirring to life in Pennepack Church in Pennsylvania a little later. During the 1680's, deacons were also becoming involved in the Baptist churches in the South. The Northern and Southern Baptists ordained these deacons.

From this new beginning the diaconate began to stir to life again. Its light began to start glowing again as the church began to believe that the authority for the diaconate came from God, the New Testament and the congregation. This belief added the necessary respect around the diaconate that was needed after its decline during the middle age.

However, since the beginning of the Reformation, two opposing views have emerged around the duties of deacons. One view contends the work of the diaconate is caring for the physical aspects of those unable to do so for themselves, but their spiritual needs were to be cared for by the pastor. Another view holds that the works of the diaconate should be both physical and spiritual.

This problem still plagues the Church today. However, a careful reading and interpretation of Holy Scripture within the context of the present cultural, and social environment will disclose many urban ministries (spiritual and temporal) for the diaconate, and all believers in Christ to practice.

Deacons should be soldiers of compassion and help in a world splintered in schisms, and live in such a way that others will emulate, and grow in Christ and servant-hood.

Chapter 4

Women And
The Diaconate

In Paul's Letter to the Church in Rome, he mentioned Phoebe as a diakonon (servant, minister) with the church at Cenchrea. This text does not tell us whether she held an office, or exactly what services she performed. The only thing we can be reasonably sure of is the time period when this letter was written. Paul wrote this letter between A.D. 55A.D.-56A.D. This would mean that Phoebe was a diakonon (minister, servant) sometimes prior to these dates. Here is what Paul says in his letter to the Church at Rome:

> *I commend to you Phoebe our sister, which is a servant of the church which is at Cenchrea: That you receive her in the Lord, as becometh saints, and that you assist her in whatever business she had need of you: for she has been a succourer of many, and of myself also.*[30]

There is no Scriptural evidence that claims she was a member of the diaconate, or that she had been ordained. But, we do know that in the church at Bythnia some of the women were designated deaconess because Pliny mentioned them in his letter on the Christians in Bythnia.

---

[30]*Rom* 16:1,2.

> *"I thought it the more necessary, therefore, to find out what truth there was in this by applying torture to two maidservants, who are called deaconesses. But I found nothing but a depraved and extravagant superstition, and I therefore postpone my examination and had recourse to you for consultation."* [31]

So, from the above citation of Pliny, we know that around the year A.D. 100, there were women in the church who were called deaconesses. We also know that they were recognized at the Council at Nice in A.D.325, and that they were certainly being **ordained** as early as the fourth century. Information in the Apostolic Constitution confirms this.

> *After she passed a careful preliminary examination the bishop was to lay hands upon her in the presence of the presbytere, deacons and other deaconesses. The bishop then ended the service with a prayer.* [32]

This information differs with the belief in many churches that deaconesses are not to be ordained. They certainly were ordained in the primitive church. It appears in light of their ordination and their relationship to the diaconate that they were ordained to a function and office. The church manual, Didascalia Apostolorum, which was written around A.D.230, provides the following information, which indicates the work of the deaconess was different from the work of the deacon. Her work was towards the women:

---

[31] Pliny (the Younger) *"Christians in Bythnia" Documents of The Christian Church* (London,1976), p.4.
[32] *Apostolic Constitution*.

> *Let a woman deacon, as we have already said, anoint the women. But let a man pronounce over them the invocation of the divine names in the water.*[33]

It appears that the role of deaconesses according to the Didascalia was auxiliary to the diaconate. They assisted the deacons and pastors in their works when women were the recipients.

The Apostolic Constitution (A.D.380), a document on church order defines the work of the deaconess as follows: 1. Keepers of the doors for women. [7:421] 2.Charity to the poor and widows. [7:430] 3.Ministry to women. [7:432]

This document also lists some of their requirements: 1. Must be virgin or if widowed married only once. 2. Must be faithful. 3. Must be held in high esteem. [7:457]

We find from the bible, ancient church manuals, and records of ancient proceedings of council meetings that at least in some cases, ordained deaconesses were used in the primitive church ministries to women.

1Timothy 3:11 is believed to be the qualifications for deaconesses. However, there is a difference of opinion on the translation of the passage. This difference is rooted in the translation of the Greek word, gynaikas and discloses whether a deaconess must be the wife of a deacon or not.

The root of gynaikas is gyne. Gyne is the word set aside for adult females. If you are speaking in a context on adult females, the word means, an adult female. If the context is about wives, the word means wife. The problem with the word as used 1Timothy 3:11 is its location within the text about deacons who were all male. There are many different biblical translations of this text. Let us look at a few of the more popular translations.

---

[33]*Didascalia Apostolorum*, trans. R. Connolly (Oxford,1929), pp.145,146.

1Timothy 3:11

King James Bible:

Even so must their wives be grave, not slanderers, sober, faithful in all things.

New International Bible:

In the same way, their wives are to be women worthy of respect, not malicious talkers but temperate and trustworthy in everything.

Amplified Bible:

[The] women likewise must be worthy of respect and serious, not gossipers, but tempered and self-controlled, [thoroughly] trustworthy in all things.

New American Standard Bible:

Women must likewise be dignified, not malicious gossips, but temperate, faithful in all things.

We can note the King James and New International Bibles translate the term as wives, while the Amplified and New American Bibles translate it to mean, women.

These various translations of the word, gynaikas informs some congregations that deacon's wives are expected to be the deaconesses of the church. Others believe that any adult woman can be a member of the deaconesses, both auxiliaries to the diaconate. A third group believes that any adult woman can be a member of the diaconate.

Those congregations that claim deaconesses are to be formed by the wives of deacons are on shakiest ground. It is so because it is not sound. Let's hypothesize and say that the chair of the diaconate has served the church for many years with faithful, and very fruitful service. His wife (deaconess) has begun to suddenly display a gossiping, and malicious personality. Should she be relieved of her position since she now, does not meet the qualifications as set forth in Paul's first Letter to Timothy? If she is relieved of her post, what impact should this have on this outstanding deacon's ministry? Should he also be relieved? It seems rather clear that if the word gynaikas is translated as wives, then the diaconate should be composed of men with their wives sharing in a team ministry. The obvious is because they have a team ministry, if one half of the team does not qualify, the other half doesn't qualify either.

This seems a little too cumbersome and shortsighted of a plan, and does not promote orderliness. We ought always do church business, *"decently, and orderly"*. This belief that gynaikas means wives, inevitably leads to the conclusion that in order to become a deacon; your wife must have the qualifications listed. A person's qualifications to the diaconate should not depend upon whether their mate qualifies or not. If that was so, many qualified and faithfully, fruitful deacons would not have become deacons and a blessing to the church in the first place.

When the word gynaikas is translated to mean the women, the passage begins to make sense in its obvious and awkward intrusion in the midst of the listing of the qualifications of deacons. I get the sense that the women are part of a group that is auxiliary to the diaconate. They are women who assist the men thereby becoming their auxiliary. Besides, there is evidence in extra-biblical writings that confirms their ministry as being exclusively to the women, whom deacons could not minister to.

Of course when the word gynaikas is translated as women it can also mean women who are part and parcel of the diaconate. This is unlikely however, because patriarchy was well and strong at this period. It is patriarchy that informs Paul's command,

> *"I suffer not a woman to teach, nor usurp authority over the man, but to learn in silence"*[34]

It informs Peter also who plainly teaches, in 1Peter 3; 1, *"Likewise, ye wives, be in subjection to your husband"*.

Under patriarchy men could have as many wives as they could care for and control. This is why Paul described one facet of the qualifications of the deacons thusly, *"Let the deacons be the husbands of one wife"* (1Tim 3:12). In a patriarchal situation, lineage and inheritance came through the male line.

The oldest son inherited all family resources. Women were held in low esteem. It was the man who ruled over the woman. For a woman to teach a man was not only unholy, but also downright rebellious and seditious against the status quo (patriarchy). Peter and Paul were both products of their time and environment. Forces that dogmatically believed in male superiority over the female formed their mindset. Their theological justification has its foundation in the creation narratives beginning at Genesis 2:4.

Some modern day mindsets that parallel the patriarchal beliefs and attitudes on patriarchy, base their beliefs on the codes of the household (above), and assemblies, *"I suffer not a woman to teach, nor usurp authority over the man..."* Some individuals, and some congregations use this as the proof text in proving women are not supposed to be members of the diaconate. This is a mistake. Paul merely says women should not teach, or have authority over men. The diaconate is not a teaching, nor overseeing ministry. Its ministry is one of compassion and helpfulness. Though the pastor may occasionally utilize the talents of some deacons in other areas of ministry, they are primarily pastors' assistants and servants of the church. Deacons are not chosen to teach and rule, but to serve and commiserate.

---

[34]*Bible*

The argument that women were not chosen to be members of the diaconate should very simply derive its impetus from the fact that the Bible never makes the claim that they were part of an office. It merely lists their qualifications (1Tim 3:11), the importance of their service, and the esteem for them, which Paul had (ROM 16:1,2). The extra-biblical literature of the church discloses a ministry of service and commiseration for the women (gynaikas) who evidently worked in some relationship with the diaconate. Their ministry however, was directed exclusively to women.

Some church literature opens historical windows on these women being ordained and set aside for their ministry. (See above: Apostolic Constitution). It appears they were *ordained* in the Church in the East to the high calling of their ministry. They worked in an assistant capacity to the deacons, caring for the women's needs. After all, they found their existence in a society that dictated their social and personal relations to men as inferior. This is pretty strong evidence that in all probability, women were not included as members of the diaconate in the ancient New Testament Church. At best they must have been members of a group that was auxiliary to the diaconate.

We must keep in mind that women (deaconesses) are and have always been, in the forefront of the struggle to proselytize the world for Jesus Christ. We must remember it was women who were the resurrection witnesses. They had the responsibility of telling the disciples that the Christ had risen from the grave (John 20:17). It was a woman who evangelized an entire town, and brought them to Jesus Christ (John 4:39). It was a woman who birthed and raised the Lord Jesus Christ (Mat 1:20,21). The Bible clearly claims the preceding facts but nowhere does it appear to claim female membership in the New Testament diaconate.

Women served faithfully in the ancient church. We discover what kinds of works they performed from such extra-biblical sources as the Apostolic Constitutions (a book on church discipline, worship and doctrine). It describes their ministry as a ministry to women.

Deaconesses were discontinued during the middle age, a time when the general diaconate was in decline and losing members to higher positions in the church. Since they could not be ordained into the priesthood as deacons could, and because they were auxiliary to the deacons, when the diaconate ended their position as deacons' assistants ended.

It appears that it was around the beginning of the 17th century, when the diaconate was being introduced into church ministries for service again, that the deaconesses began to come into the light and life of the Baptist Church once again also.

John Smyth wrote in 1607 that deacons could be male or female. He claimed the following duties for them,

> *To visit and relieve the widow, fatherless, sick, lame, blind, impotent women with child, and diseased members of the church.*[35]

In Bristol, England, sometime in the last half of the century, the Broadmead Church appointed five deaconesses to a ministry of caring for the sick and afflicted. Since this new beginning for deaconesses their responsibilities and ministries have grown, and they are contributing greatly to the New Testament Church's ever growing needs.

If your church does not have a deaconess board, you need to inform others in your congregation of their function and help organize one right away. Your church can become the recipient of the many blessed works these women can contribute to both the church, and the world within which it has physical existence.

Remember, deaconesses are not a threat to the male deacons in the area of teaching and usurping authority over them. They are no threat because the diaconate is not a teaching or

---

[35] W.T.Whitley, ed., *The Works of John Smyth*. Vol 1(Cambridge,1915), p.262.

overseeing ministry. Both these areas are quite simply the ministries of the pastor.

The church must set up training classes for the deaconesses, so as to equip them for the job and great responsibilities that go along with it. There should be a minimum of three modules for their sound training.

1.Teaching: Classroom space should be prepared and qualified personnel utilized to motivate and teach them the nuts and bolts of this ministry.

    A.   Attend Bible study, weekly.
    B.   Sunday school attendance a must

These institutions form the local church's seminary. This is where you study and show yourselves approved. This should be mandated attendance for all trainees and other Christians. When the doors open for bible study, deacons and deaconesses should form the basic attendance foundation. This is one way they can display a dedicated Christian character that others can emulate.

2.Field training: Should accompany a senior deacon to visit the sick and afflicted.

    A.   Homebound
    B.   Institutionalized

3.Internship: Each deaconess should be expected to do one of the following:

    A.   Develop a personal ministry. This can include any ministry within the Christian context of helpfulness.
    B.   Secure authority with the director of some institution to do a six-month internship with them.

After which time they are to be tested and formally set aside for the precious ministry of compassion and helpfulness.

Chapter 5

PREREQUISITES

If you were to attend a school of higher learning and wanted to enroll in certain classes of a technical nature, there would be a listing of the prerequisites you must have if you want to be a member of the class. I can recall how at seminary, I noted a class in *Old Testament Exegesis* I wanted to take. However, it was quickly brought to my attention that I needed to study and pass the Hebrew language before I could enroll in the exegesis class. Later, it became clear to me why I had to be prepared with a working knowledge of the Old Testament Hebrew language. The class including the Bible was in Hebrew. If I had been allowed to enroll in the class without successfully completing the prerequisite, I would have found myself blind and stumbling in darkness. Likewise, there are prerequisites for a person who would become a deacon or a deaconess.

The bible puts forth the following as the prerequisites for deacons, and deaconesses: should be convicted, redeemed, baptized, and understand and explain scripture to others.

1.Convicted (Romans 3:21)

All have sinned and come short of the glory of God.

By definition all Christians have been convicted. When we talk about conviction, we are really talking about reaching a place in out lives where we realize, and admit we are sinners. Because we have been convicted, we have stopped pointing at the shortcomings in other's lives and create a better atmosphere to help them. After all, we have been down that same road, and have come to realize that except by the grace of God we would still be lost on that road. Consequently, we are in a better position to help others by pointing out the potholes in the road and to come to an understanding of God and forgiveness by the blood of Jesus Christ.

What better salespersons can there be for our deliverance in Jesus Christ, than a convicted sinner? God needs convicted ex sinners to proselytize lost sinners and bring them to Him. Who can tell with better authenticity than one who has been convicted? Who can better sell the product than one who has used it and is thoroughly satisfied with its impact and performance? So in order to be a Christian deacon or deaconess, you must be convicted.

2. Redeemed (Ephesians 2:8)

For by grace are you saved through faith; and that not of ourselves.

It is the gift of God that we cannot earn on our own. We Christians must come to an understanding that we are sinful, but have been saved by the grace of God. Not because we are good or have done well, but we are saved in spite of ourselves by the unearned grace of God. We must come to know through faith that it was the blood of Jesus Christ that paid the debt in full for all of our sins. It has been correctly remarked that there are two kinds of people in the church; "lost sinners and saved sinners."

We were like condemned persons scheduled to be executed for our crimes at midnight, but someone paid the price to set us free at one second before midnight. So you see all deacons and deaconesses should be redeemed sinners. Redeemed sinners can bear witness that through redemption by Jesus Christ, you get a second chance. You get a new life to try and become what God created you to be. Deacons and deaconesses should be redeemed sinners so they can bear witness that God is a redeemer of those who are doomed.

3. Baptized (Acts 2:38)

Then Peter said unto them, repent, and be baptized every one of you in the name of Jesus Christ, for the remission of all sins, and ye shall receive the gift of the Holy Ghost.

As Christians we of necessity have been baptized. Baptism is a visible symbol of a profound change that has occurred in our spiritual being. This profound change in our lives is caused by an interaction of the Holy Spirit we called this the "Baptism of the Holy Spirit." Water baptism is a display of this spiritual occurrence. John baptized Jesus Christ in the River Jordan; therefore the Lord instituted water baptism. In our Baptist communion we practice submersion. Deacons and deaconesses should be baptized, thereby, being an example to others.

4. Understand And Explain Scripture (II Peter 3:16)

As also in his epistles, speaking in them of these things; in which are some things hard to be understood, which they that are unlearned and unstable wrest, as they do also the other scriptures to their own destruction.

If we as Christians do not understand what scripture has to say about certain things, then we are not prepared, nor qualified to teach and bring others to Christ. If we teach and don't understand, we are guilty of leading others in our own darkness. We must always be mindful of what the Bible says to us.

> *Can the blind lead the blind? Shall they not both fall in a ditch?*[36]

Deacons and deaconesses should understand, and be able to explain scripture, for after all Holy scripture tells the story of God disclosing himself in Jesus Christ and the story of the primitive church. Anyone set aside to serve in these offices and their functions are appointed to reverant places of service. And of necessity, must study and show they are,

> *...approved unto God, a workman that needeth not to be ashamed, rightly dividing the word of truth.*[37]

Adult Sunday school, and weekly Prayer and Bible Study, are the primary vehicles through which the church teaches its adult membership. This is where the Bible and church doctrine are taught. This is where our seminal tools for understanding and being able to explain God's written word comes from. Deacons and deaconesses should find their place in Sunday school, Bible Study and Prayer Meeting every time the church doors open. This way they are in a position to learn the interpretation of scripture and live and explain it to others.

---

[36] *Luke* 6:39
[37]

QUALIFICATIONS

> *Likewise must the deacons be grave, not double-tongued, not given to much wine, not greedy for filthy lucre; holding the mystery of the faith in pure conscience. And let these also first be proved: then let them use the office of deacon be found blameless...Let the deacons be the husbands of one wife, ruling their children and their own houses well.*[38]

1. Be grave: By this is meant a deacon must be dignified in dress, and attitude. He should act and talk in a manner that lifts the diaconate up. He should not get involved in acts that will lead to negative criticism of himself or, the diaconate but, should always conduct himself in a sound, Christian manner. Clowning around should never be an option.

2. He should not be double-tongued: A deacon should not be a fence straddler, saying one thing to one person, and quite the opposite of another. Deacons should always speak what they believe is the unadulterated truth.

3. Not given to much wine: Deacons should not allow wine to become their master. Remembering that you can't "serve God and Mammon."[39]

---

[38] *1 Tim* 3: 8,9,10,12.
[39] *Luke* 16:13

4. Not greedy of filthy lucre: Deacons must keep in mind that the "love of money is the root of all evil."[40] Consequently, deacons should not spend their time attempting to acquire money. Remember that Judas was a lover of money.

5. Holding the mystery of the faith in pure conscience: What is meant here is that deacons must have a strong faith. Really believing what they have confessed and profess to believe.

6. First be proved: They must show themselves as blameless. No one should have any complaint against his character, for this lofty position.

7. Be the husband of one wife: Married to one woman.

---

[40] 1 *Tim.* 6:10 b

Chapter 6

Urban Ministries

There are as many ideas about which works the diaconate is responsible for as there are denominations. Some congregations within the same denomination sometimes disagree in their ideas of deacon ministry. At times, pastors and deacons struggle against each other because of disagreement over who has responsibility for which ministry.

One method of discovering the ministries of deacons is to discover what their ministries do not include. Through the process of elimination we can arrive at their ministries.

Let us begin by allowing the Bible to define first of all, the ministry of pastors.

According to the Bible the pastor has the general oversight of the entire congregation. To have oversight is to be its earthly administrative leader. He also has the responsibility for teaching the congregation. He is the one who is called to teach the congregation.

> *The elders which are among you I exhort, who am also an elder, and a witness of the sufferings of Christ, and also a partaker of the glory that shall be revealed:*
> *Feed the flock of God which is among you, taking oversight thereof, not by constraint but willingly; not of filthy lucre, but of a ready mind.*[41]

---

[41] *1Peter* 5:1,2.

Christ is our shepherd and we are his flock. The shepherd is not here but he has left an under-shepherd to care for his flock. The congregation is God's flock and the pastor is the under-shepherd or caretaker. According to St Peter, the pastor has general oversight of the congregation. His duties include the following: preaching[42], teaching[43] and leadership.[44]

Biblically, the pastor is in charge. He is the leader and teacher of the congregation. The pastor is also the protector[45] of the flock from false doctrine and other predatory influences.

From the Bible we easily see that the diaconate is not a preaching, feeding, guiding or overseer ministry. These quite simply are ministries of the pastor.

Let us see what the Bible says about the ministry of the diaconate. If we accept Acts 6:1-6 as the proof text for the origin of deacons then lets see what it says.

> *Then the twelve called the multitude of disciples unto them and said, it is not reason that we should leave the work of God, and serve tables. Wherefore, brethren, look ye out among you seven men of honest report, full of the Holy Ghost and wisdom, whom we may appoint over this business.*[46]

The book of Acts informs us that originally deacons were appointed to supply aid to the needy. For it tells us they were to serve tables. This was in response to the Grecian Jews complaints about their widows not being taken care of as the other widows. Consequently, seven male Jews with Greek names were appointed to serve their tables. These tables were evidently tables

---

[42] *1 Tim* 5:17.
[43] *1 Tim* 3:2; Titus 1:9.
[44] Titus
[45] *1 Thes* 5:1,2
[46] *Acts* 6:2,3.

of benevolence. The church cared for the widows and deacons were set aside to serve them.

Jesus Christ is the model we should emulate if we are to continue his ministry while he sits in heaven on the right hand side of God. What does Christ say his mission was on earth?

> *The spirit of the Lord is upon me because he hath anointed me to preach the gospel to the poor; he hath sent me to heal the brokenhearted, to preach deliverance to the captives, and recovering of sight to the blind, to set at liberty them that are bruised, to preach the acceptable year of the Lord...This day this scripture is fulfilled in your ears.*[47]

Jesus is informing the persons in the synagogue, that he has come to perform a liberating ministry to a specific class of people. This ministry was focused on the *poor*, the *brokenhearted*, the *captives*, the *blind*, and the *bruised*. He was describing those who occupy the lowest rung of society, the social outcasts, those who are oppressed and dominated. Jesus claims that whatever prevents them from being whole; he will fix it and make it right. Let's observe what he says he will do in the cases listed above.

1. The poor: preach the gospel of good news to them.
2. The brokenhearted: heal them.
3. The captives: preach deliverance to them.
4. The blind: recover their sight.
5. The bruised: set at liberty.

According to our Lord, the above proclamation was his mission. If we are indeed the body of our Lord Jesus Christ, then we must make his mission our mission in today's world.

---

[47]*Luke* 4:18-21.

If deacons are to have relevant ministries in urban America, they must move to help radicalize the church so that it takes seriously the development of ministries that fall within the parameters defined by Christ around his mission. That is, ministries that seek to heal the wounds of poverty, ignorance, loneliness, and deliverance from oppression and captivity. They must seek to help design a church that parallels the New Testament Church.[48] This is the design initiated by Christ, and of necessity the design that urban deacons must help to make a reality.

Deacons are called to servant-hood, that is they are called to be the arms, and legs of God in the lives of his suffering people. The diaconate is the office of those in a servant ministry of the church. They are servants of the people. Thereby, whenever and however the people hurt, deacons through their servant-hood must seek to heal that hurt.

It is evident that the ministries of deacons are not just for those on the inside of the church edifice walls, but they must extend beyond them. How else is the unsaved going to be reached? Christ commanded us to go out and "baptize the world."[49] So, effective ministries must be designed to serve the unsaved, so they can be brought to Christ.

Let us now, look at some of the ministries that can fulfill the needs of the congregation, and also reach out to the unsaved dwellers in urban America. This list is in no way exhaustive or universal. Different localities might require ministries with a different focus. The rich and the poor have different needs asdoes the master and the slave.

1. Visitation to homes and institutions where sickness in any form is experienced.

---

[48] James.Gadsen Experiences, *Struggles and Hopes of The Black Church* (Nashville,1975), pp.10,11.
[49] Matt 28:19

2. Assist the pastor in the ordinances.

3. Benevolence: Supplying aid to those who are in dire need.

4. Stewardship: Must be good stewards, and must emphasize methods by which time, talent, and treasure concept is materialized in the membership.

5. Mid-week prayer meeting.

6. Lay preaching: As determined by the pastor.

7. Evangelism: Ministries of relevance to its constituents.

    A. Substance abusers.
    B. Programs designed to save the youth.
    C. Prison ministries.
    D. A.I.D.S. sufferers.
    E. Unwed teenage mothers programs.
    F. Programs that teach self-respect and personal growth.
    G. Manage all auxiliaries. Choir, Usher Board, etc.

Visitations to the Sick and Afflicted:

1. Home Visitations
2. Institutional Visitations
  A. Hospitals
  B. Group Care and, Board and Care Facilities

When members of the congregation have physical or spiritual needs, deacons should visit them with the spiritual, objective of uplifting them and caring for their needs. When one member is suffering from any form of broken-ness, the whole congregation suffers. The Bible informs us of the following.

> *That there should be no schism in the body; but that the members should have the same care one for another. And when one member suffer, all the members suffer with it; or one member be honoured, all the members rejoice with it. Now you are the body of Christ, and members in particular.*[50]

Visiting the sick is one of the primary ministries of the diaconate. These visitations are made with the objective of reassuring and uplifting the sufferer. Any verbalizations should be uplifting in spirit and effect, and grounded in Jesus Christ. These visits are by necessity, short and dignified. Gossiping has no place in these or any Christian visitations.

Visits to the homes of those who are sick should be conducted in a dignified manner and, an appointment should be made. This is not a social call but a call of compassion to a sister or, brother in their time of broken-ness. This is a call to heal, not a call to gossip. This is a call to reassure and, lift up the sick person through scripture and prayer. If the sick person can understand and answer you it is in good taste to ask whether it is all right to read scripture or pray. Be considerate and do not try to sound impressive with the use of long prayers and reading a long scripture that doesn't speak to the occasion. You should determine which scripture you are going to share before you make the visit. You should also read the scripture several times before attempting to read it to someone else.

Skilled Nursing facilities, and Group Care Homes can be visited on a regular basis. These visits should be made prayerfully. It is best if teams comprised of a male and female make these visits. Some ministries include bible study or, praise periods for some of the residents at regular intervals. Contact should be made with the director of nursing to get her approval for your team to provide a ministry to the residents. This can be a

---

[50] 1*Cor* 12:25.

very rewarding Christian experience as your ministry of compassion begins to help them bear their burden more hopefully.

ORDINANCES

1. Baptism:

Deacons are to assist the pastor in the ritual of baptism. A pastor or ordained minister should administer the rite when available, but when an emergency exists and, a pastor or minister cannot be secured to officiate, a deacon can be authorized to administer the function. After all, when Philip met the Ethiopian official who requested baptism, he performed it when no minister was present.

> *And as they went on their way, they came unto a certain water: and the eunuch said, See, here is water; what doth hinder me to be baptized? And Philip said, If thou believest with all thine heart, thou mayest. And he answered and said, I believe that Jesus Christ is the Son of God. And he commanded the chariot to stand still: and they went down into the water, both Philip and the eunuch; and he baptized him.*[51]

Normally, deacons and deaconesses should assist the pastor, whose function it is to administer this ordinance, by making sure the pool has been prepared and the all other particulars associated with baptism are taken care of properly.

Deaconesses should be on hand to assist the female candidates prepare and receive this ordinance.

---

[51] *Acts* 8:37.

It is important that deacons and deaconesses present themselves in such a way that the holiness and importance of baptism is mirrored.

2. The Lord's Supper

Deacons should assist the pastor or minister in this ordinance by serving the congregation. Deaconesses should assist by preparing the elements and everything associated with this ordinance. The Bible does not inform us to how regular, or how often this ordinance should be performed.

In our communion (Baptist Church), we serve the Lord's Supper on the First Sunday and on special occasions.

The role of the diaconate in this celebration is to first, make sure the altar and elements have been properly, prepared; second, distribute the elements to the believers, and third, see to it that the remains of the celebration are properly cared for.

The meaning of The Lord's Supper is in its symbolism of the bread representing the body of our crucified Savior, and the wine his blood. With the total celebration being one whose purpose it is to remember the Lord's death, until his Second Coming.

The meaning of the ordinance of Baptism is in its symbolism of death of the old, and the birth of the new Christian self. Deacons and deaconesses should assist the pastor in this ritual and also provide proper preparation for the baptismal pool and all of the necessities of this ritual.

These ordinances are rituals of high holiness and should be celebrated in a most reverent manner.

Benevolence:

Deacons' importance in the New Testament Church today, must find its place in their caring for the needy, poor and those suffering, in a Christ centered manner. After all this is why the deacon was brought into being. The deacon was created to fill a vital church need according to Acts 6:2; "it is not desirable for us to neglect the word of God in order to serve tables". The apostles were prioritizing their ministries at a time when the church was experiencing rapid membership growth. They needed help in conducting its ministries. The original "seven" were appointed to care for the tables of the poor widows.

This ministry to the poor and needy community is thoroughly grounded in the Bible. We read the apostle Paul stating in his letter to the Corinthians,

> *And though I bestow all of my goods to feed the poor, and though I give my body to be burned, and have not charity, it profiteth me nothing.*[52]

Deacons should be responsible for dispersing of these funds. This is a ministry that can impact dramatically on the recipient's life, if it is taken seriously to its ultimate conclusion in Jesus Christ. This ministry should have as its goal, the relieving of the poverty these persons experience in their daily lives. After all, in the fourth chapter of Luke our Savior claims he came to loose the chains that bind.

Deacons have an opportunity in this service, to practice a ministry that will enhance the liberation of the poor from what binds them. They must keep in mind that "giving a person a fish when he is hungry is a good thing, but to teach that person how to fish" is to liberate them from what binds them.

---

[52] *1 Cor* 13:3.

Stewardship

Stewardship is the act of managing what belongs to someone else. In the Christian use of the term, its significance is in the management of God's world, and everything in it.

It is important that each person affiliated with the diaconate be a good steward. They must strive at all times to keep their best foot forward in being flesh and blood examples of their time, talent, and treasures being used for the Lord. Many members of a congregation utilize members of the diaconate as their role models. It is of grave importance that deacons through their behavior encourage others to be good stewards. They should always remember that the lives the congregation sees them living, will be their most influential teaching tool.

Lay Preaching

If a deacon indicates a gift for preaching, then by all means he should be afforded the opportunity to exercise this gift on special occasions. After all, Deacon Stephen of the primitive church has already blazed a trail that leads to preaching by the diaconate. However, deacons are not set aside to preach, but may exercise this gift with the approval of the pastor.

Prayer Meeting

It is very important for the continued uplifting of the believers, that a mid-weekly, prayer meeting takes place. This is needed because by mid- week some of us are coming down from the exhilaration of Sundays' worship service. The mid-weekly prayer meeting should provide enough spiritual nourishment to help us make it through until Sunday.

It is the diaconate's responsibility to secure the presence of as many persons as possible for prayer meeting, and to have oversight over it.

Evangelism

Evangelism is the act of winning lost souls to Christ.

Jesus Christ commands us to "*go ye therefore*" and bring all peoples into the fold. (Matt 28:19) It is imperative that the diaconate develops some plans for reaching the un-saved of the world. They must look around and see, and feel the pain, and anguish of those who suffer in Urban America. Once they feel this pain, they will be in a better position to develop programs whose goals are to relieve that pain. It will present an excellent opportunity to witness for Christ's sake as he commands us.

If urban dwellers are to be evangelized, relevant ministries must reach out to them. If their hurts and concerns are addressed the evangelist has a better chance of winning them for Christ. It is only by reaching out that deacons will be able to grasp a hand to pull into the fold.

If the unsaved are to be won for Jesus Christ, ministries to reach them must be developed. The following are some suggestions:

Substance Abusers

There are far too many substance abusers in our urban communities. If we don't get a grip on this one we could lose it all. There are many crimes associated with this satanic, industry in our midst. Deacons must come to an understanding that the only drug program that can truly liberate the abuser is the drug program of Jesus Christ. Once this reality sets in, a way to get the abuser to hear and understand your witness about what Christ has done for you, and how he is willing to help them must be planned. A program that addresses their problems and needs must be developed if these people are to be helped.

Youth Programs

Our youth in urban America are the most important asset for our future. If our youth are lost, our future is lost. To hold back the tide of destruction that is sweeping our children into spiritual, mental, and physical death, we must reach out to them with programs that fill their needs, and eradicates their low self-esteem. Programs must be set up that make them proud to be humans, and leads to their acceptance of Jesus Christ as their Lord and savior.

Prison Ministry

Jesus states in the fourth chapter of Luke, that he had come to ***"preach deliverance to the captives."*** If we are in Christ and Christ is in us, then we must be about doing his ministries to a sin, sick world. Deacons need to become involved in ministries to prisoners, preaching the theology of deliverance to them.

Aids Victims

When we read the gospel writer's depiction of Jesus' life, we often find Jesus taking time to help those who suffered from physical sickness. Aids sufferers need care, and deacons would be continuing the ministry of Jesus Christ, if they would stop for a while and realize that caring for the sick has continually been a ministry of the diaconate.

Unwed Teenage Mothers

There is a tremendous need for the deaconesses, mothers, and deacons to begin to seriously look at programs that can teach our boys, and girls how to develop values that will move towards elimination of actions that stem from bad judgment. Since pregnancy is a male and female endeavor, a program should be developed that addresses their sexual and Christian responsibility. The church must care about the well being of the whole person physically, spiritually, and mentally.

Mentoring Programs

There are many young boys that fail to be motivated because there aren't any positive male role models in their lives. Their role models are drug dealers, gangsters, pimps, hustlers, abusers of women and other negative personalities. Deacons could set up programs composed of men who are positive, and successful in some way, and agree to spend some time with a youth. Hopefully, through association the youth will accept the adult male as a role model and begin to emulate him. Of course our main goal is to proselytize the youth and win him/her for Jesus Christ, who is the answer to all the problems our youth are facing in urban America. First however, we have to persuade them to listen before our witnessing can impact effectively upon them. The program must get their attention.

Programs That Enhance Self Respect

Deacons should be involved with programs for all age groups in an urban congregation that teaches growth in love of self, and for others.

All Auxiliaries

All auxiliary ministries are the responsibilities of the diaconate. The laymen, ushers, music department, prayer, praise, etc., are examples of ministries that should be within the scope of diaconate responsibility.

Good News Of Rewards For Faithful Service

> *For they that have used the office of a deacon well purchase to themselves a good degree, and great boldness in the faith which is in Jesus Christ.*[53]

The Bible informs us that if deacons serve well they will find the Lord faithful and purchase for themselves a very solid foundation of boldness in Jesus Christ on which to stand. This is where the real power of deacons derives from.

---

[53] 1*Tim* 3:13.

Some Notable Deacons of The Past

Callistus, (160-222). He was born a slave and advanced up the church heirachy from deacon to pope.

St Athanasia, (293-373). Ordained a deacon, served as secretary to the bishop of Alexander. Formulated the Homoousian Doctrine.

St. John Chrysostom, (349-407.) Church Father, ordained a deacon in 381, and priest in 386.

St. Beder. The Venerable, (673-735) Benedictine monk and scholar. Ordained a deacon, and later a priest.

St. Edmund, (1540-1581) Martyred during reign of Queen Elizabeth 1. Ordained a deacon in 1567.

George Berkeley, (1685-1753). Founder of the modern school of idealism. Ordained a deacon in 1567.

John Wesley, (1703-1791). Ordained a deacon in 1725.

George Whitfield, (1714-1770). Ordained a deacon in the Church of England in 1736.

50

Some Notable Deacons of The Past

St. Philip, (160-222). He was born a slave and ordained up Deacon. Church believed by Francis Deacon to pope.

Bishop Ignatius, (235-322). Ordained a deacon, served as secretary to the bishop of Alexander. Formulated the Homoosian Doctrine.

St. John Chrysostom, (c.1600?). Liturgy. Church Father ordained a deacon in 381, and priest in 386.

St. Bede, The Venerable, (673-735). Benedictine monk and scholar, ordained a deacon, and later a priest.

St. Edmund, (1340-1521). Martyred alongside nuns of Queen Elizabeth I. Ordained a deacon in 1569.

Thomas Gresley, (1655-1735). Founder of the modern school of surgeon. Ordained deacon in 1700.

John Wesley (1703-1771). Ordained a deacon in 1725.

Thomas Wyatt, (1422-1542). Exiled, abolished a deacon in the Church of 1746.

Chapter 7

ROLE OF A MOTHERS' BOARD

There should be a Mothers' Board operating within each church family in the African American Church, for two reasons: First, reverence for the wise, aged female has deep historical roots in our African culture, and our people need them now, more than ever. Especially since we are losing generations of our youths to gangs, prisons, drugs, under-achievement and death. We need those women who are wise from experience and study to be the mother role model to the congregation and help instill the correct values in our people; second, we need them because of their ability to nurture the members of the congregation.

In our traditional African cultures we have always revered and respected the elders of our community. Our elders are closer to our ancestors than we are. They are our connections to the past. Since they have traveled further on the journey of life, they can better point out the potholes and other obstacles we will encounter. Because we lost respect for them and what they stood for, we have lost respect for ourselves.

There is a direct correlation between our loss of respect and honor for our elders and the depravity we find ourselves in today. The most revered of our elders are our mothers. Mothers in African and African/American consciousness have occupied a place of reverence that is superseded only by our love for God. We need Mothers' Board members who can live and act in a way that we can revere and listen to for advice, and by their example get a grip on our lives.

QUALIFICATIONS

Women of the Mothers' Board are appointed to a very lofty ministry in the church. Consequently, they should be devout Christian women. They should not be given to gossip, dishonesty, malice, enviousness, hatred, deceitfulness, jealousy, or indecent dress.[54]

Mothers must realize that they are called to fill a special, and exalted role that differs from all others in the church. They are the Church Mothers. We must remember that the church is the bride of Christ. In a sense the mothers of the church are the mothers of the bride of Christ. When God calls to great roles in ministry, He requires great responsibility. Anyone felt called to this great ministry should meet the following qualifications: They must study to show themselves approved and held in high esteem by the church; They must live a sanctified Christian life and project a Christ-like character; They must show themselves friendly and possess a gracious personality. They must have a sympathetic heart; they must be appropriate in appearance and immaculate in dress. They must display a happy disposition. They must not engage in talk or do things that stunt the enhancement and growth of others in Christ. They must be full of wisdom and ready to share that wisdom and the gospel of Jesus Christ with others for their growth.

They must understand and publicly express their love and obligations to the pastor so they can teach it to others.[55] They must also possess a basic, working knowledge of church administration.

The above qualifications combined with being convicted (Romans 3:21), redeemed (Ephesians 2:8), baptized (Acts2: 38), and understand and explain Scripture to others (II Pet 3:16).

---

[54] *Titus* 2:3-5
[55] *Hebrew* 13:7

RESPONSIBILITIES

1. Teach women what it means to be God fearing, moral leaders in their families,[56] churches and communities. Many of the women in our communities and churches have low self-esteem. This negative self-perception is a legacy of slavery. Our people however, cannot rise any higher than our women. Consequently, our women must be elevated so they can be the lighthouses pointing us towards higher levels of existence.

2. Teach female youth what it means to be respectful, honors due, African/American women. Then as they mature they will stand on a firm foundation, ready to move our race and others to higher levels in Jesus Christ.[57]

3. Teach and encourage the female children how to be, and act lady-like (in Christ), etc. There should be classes on hygiene, poise, and perhaps rights of passage etc.[58]

4. Practice and teach support of the pastor. The pastor deserves and needs your spiritual support[59] and should also be supported monetarily.[60] Mothers should do all that can be done, especially by example, to convince the congregation and individuals to support the pastor. In this life, with its troubling times, there is no substitute for a caring pastor. A caring pastor is always there when you need him, and becomes an enhancer in your recovery. On more occasions than you perhaps realize, he has served you when he was suffering himself. He prays for you consistently and deserves your support.

---

[56] *Proverbs* 14:1
[57] *Titus* 2:4
[58] *Proverbs* 22:6
[59] I *Thessalonians* 5:12,13
[60] I *Corinthians* 9:2-15

5. Visit and pray for the sick and afflicted, and other deaconess ministries. Regular visits should be made to *homes* and *institutions*. These visits should be dignified in manner, non gossiping and of a reasonable time limit. You are called to leave a blessing not pain.

6. Other ministries as determined by the pastor and congregation according to your gifts and graces.

ORGANIZATION

This board should consist of a president, vice president, secretary and treasurer. This board is essentially an advisory board.

The President: Should open and close the meetings promptly at the hours appointed. She should moderate the business meetings. While she is not entitled to make a motion she may call attention to any particular business that should be brought before the board. She should keep careful oversight over the work of the other mothers.

Vice President: Be acquainted with all the duties of the president, and be prepared to preside in her absence. She should cooperate with the president in the accomplishment of the purpose of the board.

Secretary: Must keep a correct record of the proceedings of the meetings. Note all resolutions, motions, and amendments. Her duties also include: 1.Keeping a roll of members; 2.Call the roll at Meetings; 3. Read aloud all resolutions to be brought before the board.

Treasurer: 1.Receive all moneys, 2.Keep a correct account of the sources of income. 3.Keep a list of members and dates of payment of dues. Provide financial reports as required.

All Members: Obligations are as follows: participation in the ministries of the Mothers Board, and congregation.

MISCELLANEOUS MINISTRIES

Prayer Warriors: These women should fast and pray and display love for the church. The prayer warrior should live a consecrated life and be able to connect and communicate with God at anytime and anyplace. These women must be able to comfort those in need and enhance the strength of those who are weak. They should have the faith to believe that God answers prayer.

Prayer and Bible Band: This ministry provides for the training of women to know the Bible and become knowledgeable in God's Word, so they can help lead lost souls to Jesus Christ. A Bible band can help the ministry of women become more successful, and teach them what God wants them to do. The Bible Band presents the opportunity for teaching women how to love and care for their husbands in a Christ centered way. It can become an excellent evangelical tool, when done within the context of various neighborhood satellites.

Periodical Meeting With All Women: Mothers should meet with all the women of the church and teach them those things that will enhance their womanhood and consequently, make them better servants of the family, church, community, and God.

If this board is to be effective it must have the blessings of the pastor and congregation. Ineffectiveness of this board will act as a barrier to the progress of the church. This board if dedicated to the ministries appointed them could make the difference in building a successful, caring church and a failure by the side of the road.

THE PRIMARY MINISTRIES

The number one ministry for the Mothers Board is the same as it is for all Christians. Their first responsibility is to worship and give praise to God. This quite literally means they must attend worship service consistently, providing their health allows. Along with this ministry, Mothers must seek out the lost and bring them to Christ. Jesus Christ in his last command, claimed and demanded,

> All power is given unto me in heaven and in earth. Go ye therefore, and teach all nations, baptizing them in the name of the Father, and of the Son, and of the Holy Ghost.[61]

While the above listed ministries should be performed, bringing lost souls to Jesus Christ is the one ministry that Christ commissioned us (Christians) to practice. The function of all ministries of the church is to provide a door by which the lost can be brought into the fold, and an encounter with Christ.

To be a witness for Christ is a process of two parts: First, You should live righteously, because your Christian life depicted for the unsaved will display for them, someone who has been saved by Jesus, secondly, you must testify with your lips. Fishing for and bringing in lost souls is your great task. Workshops should be provided to teach you how to approach a prospect, how to present your message, and how to close the net. You have been called to be a soldier in the Lord's army.

---

[61] *Matthew* 28:18,19

WOMAN, MOTHER OF ALL

In ancient societies a woman's place was not one of oppression, or secondary to men. Ancient men* realized that a woman's function in childbirth brought her into intimate association with the mystery of life, and he accepted the fact that a mother was special. He could not give birth, nor could he understand what were its causes. So women were revered as producers of life. During this period descent flowed through the mother since the biological role played by the father in birth was unknown.

As mother, and Matriarch, she presided over a pattern of life that she accepted. It was her proper domain, made glorious by the was of primary importance; she had little time for self-pity, and was less inclined to break faith with her sacred trust, Motherhood.

As home making departed from the hut, and moved to the house, she found further demands upon her energies. She must have prided herself upon a well ran home, during a time when there were no household gadgets. A mans' position in life was symbolized by the station of his wife and the good breeding of her children. It was women who founded agriculture and consequently, civilization itself. Woman was recognized as the Mother, and the producer of life and a better way for all.

Let us look at today. In the African/American families, the mother still occupies a central role that is closely related to the matriarchy in our motherland, Africa. When we speak of a family's home, we say Mary's, or Bessie's house. We give this same recognition to the children; they are always the mother's children. The mother does most of the molding of the child morally and psychologically. The father and environment act mostly as modifiers of what the mother has taught. When we were adhering to this setup, our children came out of the family

---

* Early Nile Valley occupants.

structure and moved more or less successfully in some of their endeavors in the American system. As we have turned our backs on the sanctity of motherhood, we have lost the initiative, motivation and hope to make our mark in this society.

If we are to get back on the right track again we will definitely need mothers, who deserve praise and, reverence that will result in our lives having a more positive outlook. We need older, wiser women (Mothers Board) to teach our potential mothers how to gain the respect they deserve from all.

Men may rule the world, but because of their holy intimacy with life itself women must give birth to a better kind of world on the spiritual and physical level.

FEMALE BIBLICAL ROLE MODELS

RUTH: The book of Ruth begins with sorrow (bereavement), and ends with happiness. These are the two aspects of all human life. Satisfaction and discontentment, hope and disappointment, achievement and failure, joy and sorrow, follow every human being through life. These two aspects are dealt with in the Book of Ruth.

ESTHER: The woman whose courage saved a nation. Her statement exemplified this courage "If I perish I perish." This woman had the courage to seek the favor of the king's scepter, in spite of the law, because of her trust in the providence of God. She had a dependence on God. By her actions Israel was saved. The Book of Esther tells us of the diplomacy by which she approached Ahasuerus and implicated Haman in the terrible plot for her destruction and the destruction of her people. As God did for the Jews under Esther, He is able to do for us today.

MARY: The noblest woman of all. She is called, "The mother of our Lord." She is called, "Blessed among women." She never deserted Jesus. She was at his trial, his scourging, and his crucifixion, she was with him to the end.

DORCAS: She was a woman full of good works. "All the widows stood by him weeping, and showing the coats and garments which Dorcas had made." (Acts 9:39)

LYDIA: The contrast between vision and reality is great. Nowhere is this brought out more clearly than between Paul's vision of the man of Macedonia and Paul's first convert in Europe, the woman Lydia. She was a woman with an open heart.

THE STEWARDSHIP PARABLES OF JESUS CHRIST

The Rich Fool...Luke 12:16-21
Dives and Lazarus...Luke 16:19-32
The Prodigal...Luke 15:11-32
The Talents...Matthew 25:14-30
The Pounds...Luke 19:11-2
The Judgment...Matthew 25:31-4
The God Samaritan...Luke 10:25-37
The Ten Virgins...Matthew 25:1-1
The Householder...Matthew 20:1-1
The Wicked Husbandman...Matthew 21:33-45
The Unprincipled Steward...Luke 16:1-12

HOW TO SUCCEED IN CHRISTIAN LIFE

1. Rely upon the Holy Spirit. Ephesians 5:18; Acts 1:8
2. Confess Jesus as Lord. Romans 10:9,10; Philemon 2:11
3. Pray without ceasing. 1 Thessalonians 5:17-Luke 18:1
4. Search the scriptures daily. John 5:39; Acts 17-11
5. Attend public worship regularly. Hebrews 10:25; Psalms 50:5
6. Give liberally without grudging. ll Corinthians 9:7; Luke 6:38
7. Give attention to missions. John 4:45-36; Matthew 28:19-20
8. Forget self-live for others. Matthew 20:26-28; 1 John 3:16
9. Witness to someone daily. Acts 2:42,46,47
10. Keep growing in grace. II Peter 3:18; Ephesians 4:12-16
11. Memorize one verse daily. Psalms ll9; Ephesians 4:12,16
12. Carry your Bible or Testament with you always. Titus 1:9; Phil.2:16

QUESTIONS

1. What is a servant?

2. What is a minister?

3. Are all Christians ministers?

4. What is a deacon?

5. Where is the origin and authority for deacons found in the Bible?

6. What were they authorized to do?

7. Were they ordained?

8. What are the qualifications for deacons?

9. What is a deaconess?

10. Where is the origin and authority for deaconess found?

11. Were they ordained?

12. What are the qualification for deaconesses

13. How does the diaconate relate to the pastor?

14. Who has oversight of the congregation?

15. What did Jesus Christ claim as his mission in the Gospel of Luke?

16. Are we responsible for making the ministry of Christ functional in believers' lives? How do we do this?

17. What did Jesus mean when he talked about doing His Fathers business?

TRAINING PROGRAM

Deacons, Deaconesses, and Mothers:

Teaching. Classroom space and qualified personnel should be utilized to motivate, and teach the nuts and bolts of this precious ministry.

1. TEACHING

A. Attend Bible study, weekly. Every church is it's own seminary. If we are to be trained it is of utmost importance that we attend Sunday school and Bible study, regularly. Church Seminary attendance is a must. It is within Sunday school and Bible Study where materials will be covered that relate to acquiring an understanding of biblical scripture in preparation for ordination examination. Besides the bible informs us we should "study to show ourselves approved." (prerequisite)

B. Attend a six-month, monthly class on the origin, qualifications, and ministry of deacons, deaconesses, and mothers. Some of the areas to be covered will include the following.

    C. Denominational Polity
        1. Autonomous nature of the Baptist Church.
        2. Context and function of the Bay Area Baptist District Assoc
        3. Context and function of State Convention

    D. Pastor's/ Deacon's Roles.

    E. Deacon Family Ministry Plan

    F. Pastoral Functions
        1.Baptism. It's symbolism, including the

difference between infant Baptism, and believer's Baptism.
2. Lord's Supper. It's symbolism, and why we celebrate.
3. Assisting the family through the grieving process.

2. FIELD TRAINING

A. Institutional Visitation. How to? Check in procedures, what to, and not do. Hospitals, Nursing Homes, SNFs, Jails, Prisons, and etc.

C. Home Visitations

3. INTERNSHIP

A. Six month internship at Institution, or concretize a personal ministry

4. PERSONAL ISSUES

A. My salvation experience.
B. My Calling

BASIC GUIDE LINES FOR VISITING INSTITUTIONS

Prisons, Jails, Hospitals, Nursing Homes, Court Rooms, etc.

Why Should You:

    Know the visiting hours?

    Know the rules for visitation

    Follow the institutional rules as closely as possible

    Remember to "check-in" @the desk, booth, etc.

Basically, so you do not cause a disturbance and get into trouble, therefore causing the person you are attempting to visit trouble!

Remember your purpose for being there! You are there to represent Christ! Therefore, say a prayer, and read a scripture. Listen as much as possible in a non-judgmental manner. Leave after 15-20 minutes.

    Should you give legal or medical advice?

    Should you "second guess" institutional professionals?

    Could you get into trouble by breaking the rules?

Why should you know when to leave, especially in ICU settings! *(Most ICU's have rules limiting visitors, and how long they can stay!)*

    Why would you want to meet with the family in the waiting room? *(The ICU could be crowded with family members, or medical personnel)*

Funeral Assistance

    1. Call family and ask if they want a visit, prayer or both. Do more listening than anything else. Read a scripture, have prayer and leave.
    2. If doing contract work, be godly and professional.
    3. If not doing contract work, do a lot of listening
    4. Offer to accompany them to the mortuary.

Denominational Issues

    1. How do Baptists understand the local church? *(It is free of all outside interference, and loyal ultimately to Christ)*

    2. What is the next level of participation? (District)

    3. What is the next level of participation? *(The State Baptist Convention)*

    4. What is the next level of participation? *(The National Baptist Convention, USA, Inc.)*

Biblically speaking, Should you participate in running down the reputation of your church or pastor? Should the pastor be obeyed? *(Hebrews 13:17).*

BIBLIOGRAPHY

Agar. F.F. *The Deacon at Work*. Valley Forge: 1923.

Bettenson, Henry. ed. *Documents of the Christian Faith*. London 1976.

DeWeese, Charles. *The Emerging Role of Deacons*, Nashville:1979.

Connolly, R.translator. *Didascalia Apostolorum* Oxford: 1929.

Eusebius. *The History of the Church*. Trans. G. Williamson. New York: 1965.

Gadsen, James. *Experiences, Struggles and Hopes of the Black Church*. Nashville: 1975.

Dudley, Dean. *History of the Council of Nice* New York:1922.

Hitchcock, Roswell. *Hitchcock's Topical Bible*. Grand Rapids:1969

Holmes,Urban. *The Future Shape of Ministry*. NY:1971.

Holy Bible. editions: *Amplified*; *King James;*
New American Standard Bible

Kee, Howard. *Understanding the New Testament*.3rd edit. New Jersey: 1973.

Lost Books of The Bible & The Forgotten Books of Eden. 1974.

Massey, Floyd. *Church Administration In The Black Perspective*.
Valley Forge: 1964.

Nichols, Harold. *The Work of The Deacon and Deaconess*.
Valley Forge: 1964.

Strauch, Alexander. *The New Testament Deacon*. Colorado:1992.

The International Standard Bible Encylopedia. 5Vol. Grand Rapids:1939.

The Wycliff Bible Commentary. Chicago:1962.

The Wycliff Bible Encyclopedia. Chicago: 1975.

www.ingramcontent.com/pod-product-compliance
Lightning Source LLC
Chambersburg PA
CBHW051703090426
42736CB00013B/2512